THIS BOOK BELONGS TO

_____

TO ALL THE LITTLE TRAIN LOVERS
AND THEIR AMAZING ADVENTURES!

Eddie's mum was a hardworking nurse. Despite her busy schedule, she always made time for him. They would share their stories over dinner, and Eddie would tell her about his latest train adventures. At night, he dreamed of the rhythmic chug of engines and riding the fastest trains to faraway places.

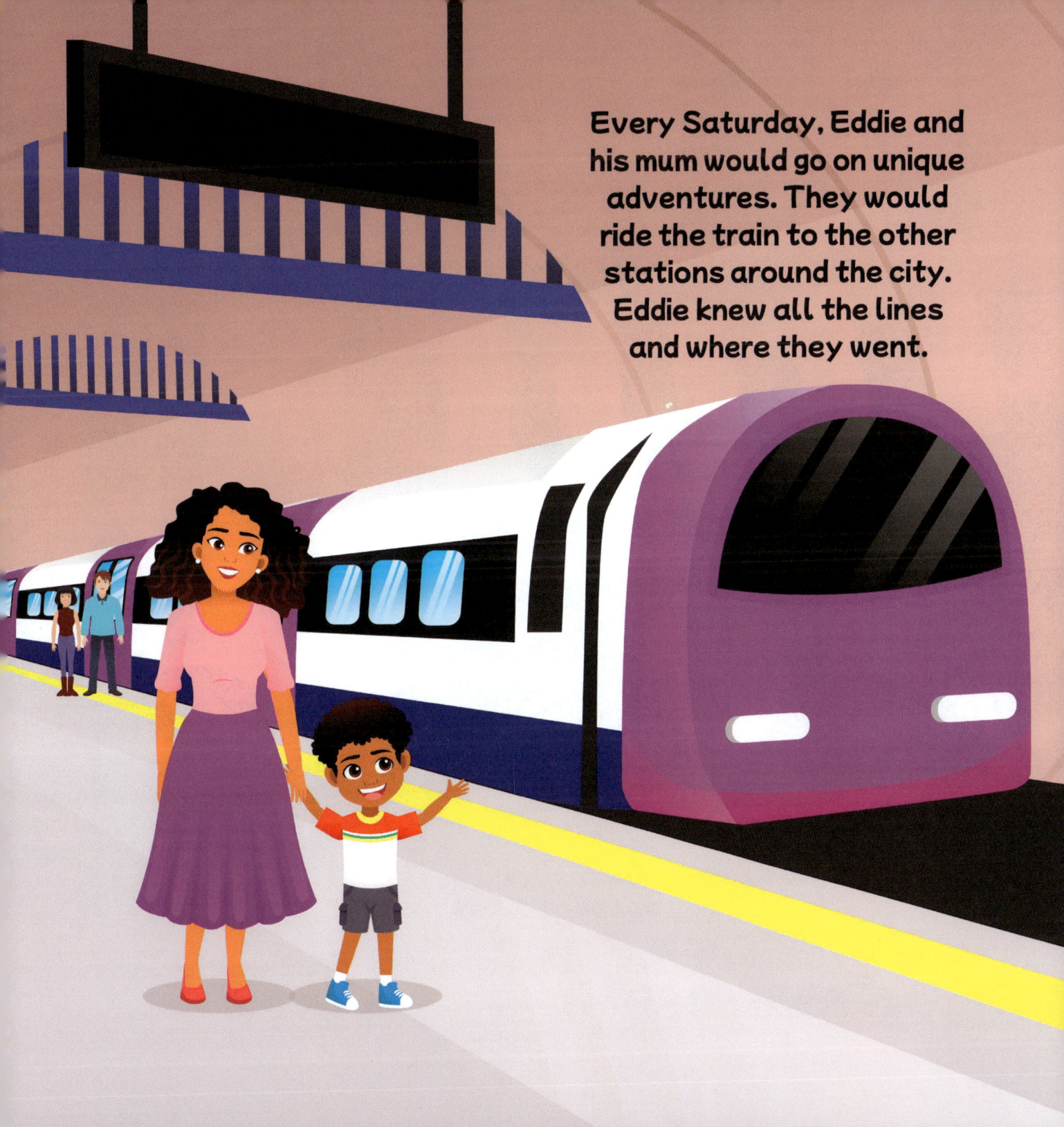

Every Saturday, Eddie and his mum would go on unique adventures. They would ride the train to the other stations around the city. Eddie knew all the lines and where they went.

During the adventures, Eddie marvelled at the real trains as they whooshed by, their wheels clattering on the tracks. He would imagine himself aboard a magnificent locomotive bound for magical lands.

Eddie and his mum visited the City Transport Museum on a sunny Saturday afternoon in July. He eagerly explored the collection of taxis, buses, motor cars, trams, locomotives, and trains. His eyes sparkled with excitement.

Eddie enjoyed his time at the museum; he climbed aboard an old steam locomotive. He got to pull the whistle cord and pretend he was driving the train. "All aboard!" he shouted happily.

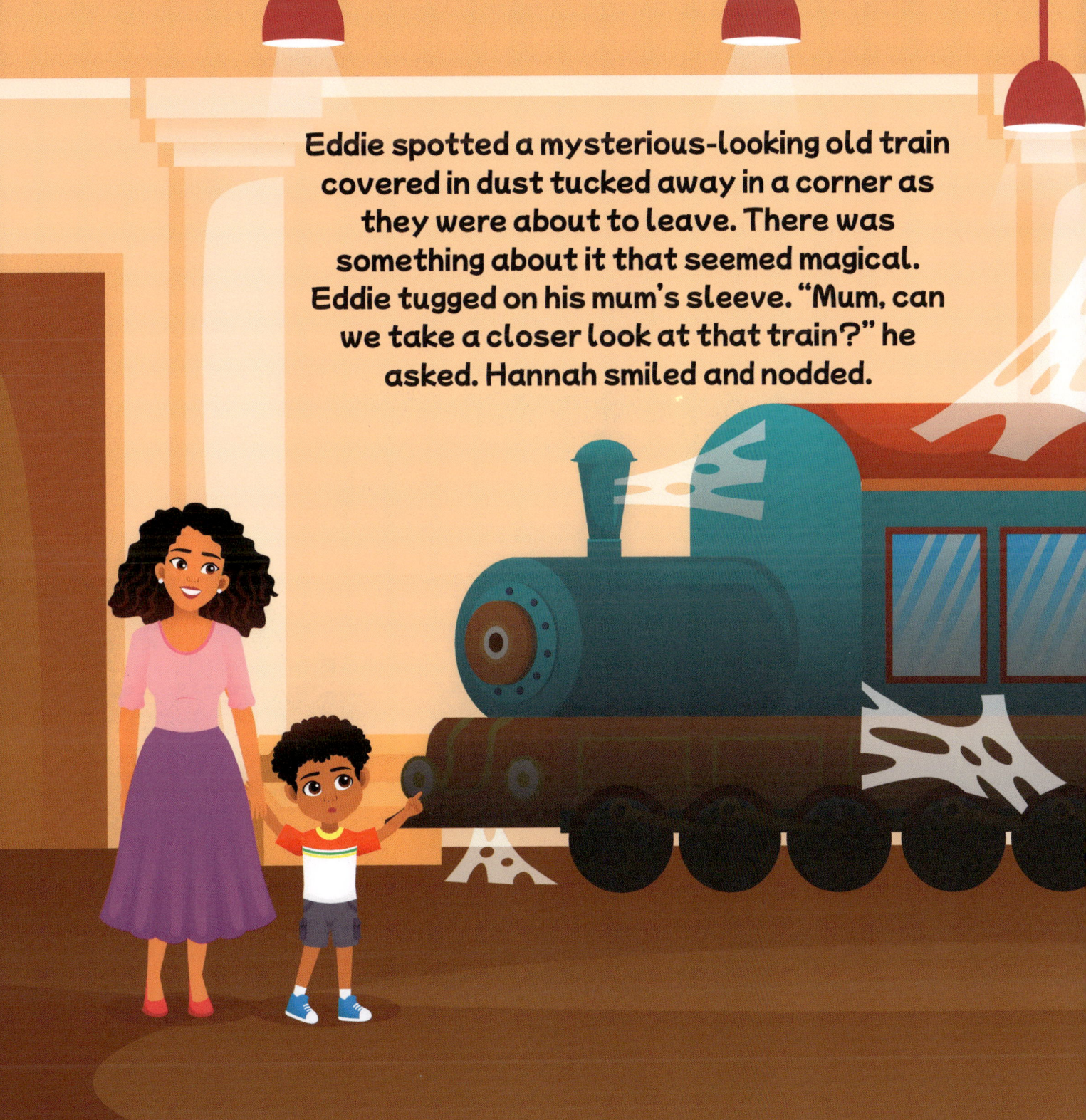

Eddie spotted a mysterious-looking old train covered in dust tucked away in a corner as they were about to leave. There was something about it that seemed magical. Eddie tugged on his mum's sleeve. "Mum, can we take a closer look at that train?" he asked. Hannah smiled and nodded.

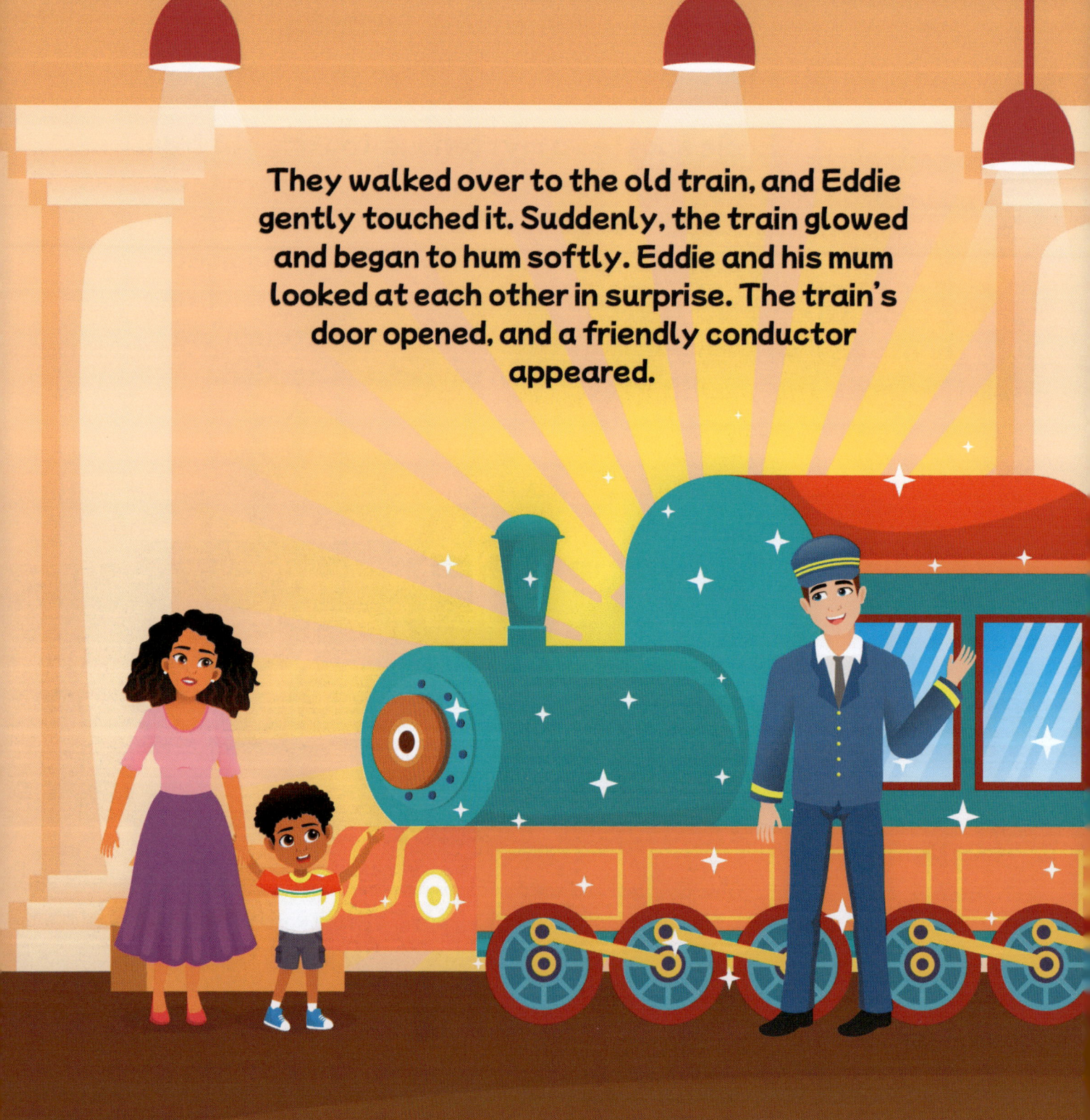
They walked over to the old train, and Eddie gently touched it. Suddenly, the train glowed and began to hum softly. Eddie and his mum looked at each other in surprise. The train's door opened, and a friendly conductor appeared.

"Hello, Eddie! I'm Mr. Conductor," he said. "This is the Adventure Express. It can take you anywhere you wish to go. Would you like to come aboard for an epic train ride?"

Eddie's heart raced with excitement. "Yes, please!" he exclaimed. Hannah, though a little unsure, agreed to join the exciting journey.

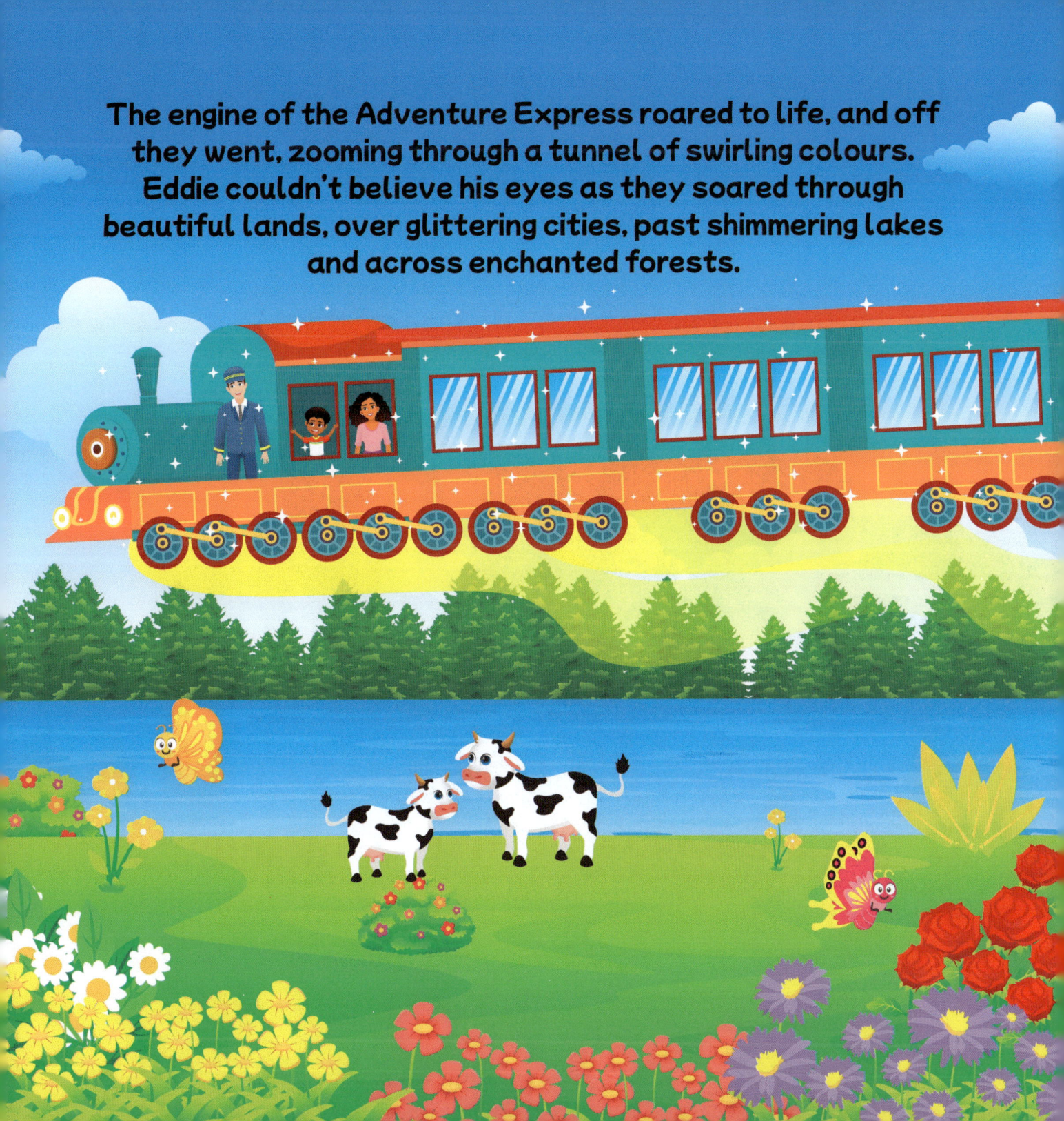

The engine of the Adventure Express roared to life, and off they went, zooming through a tunnel of swirling colours. Eddie couldn't believe his eyes as they soared through beautiful lands, over glittering cities, past shimmering lakes and across enchanted forests.

Eddie and his mum were captivated by the talking animals. Ella the Fox was clever and playful, Oli the Elephant was gentle and strong, Abi the Cat was mischievous yet charming, and Perri the Parrot was vibrant and chatty. Each animal brought unique skills and wisdom, helping Eddie uncover the train's mysteries and forge unforgettable memories.

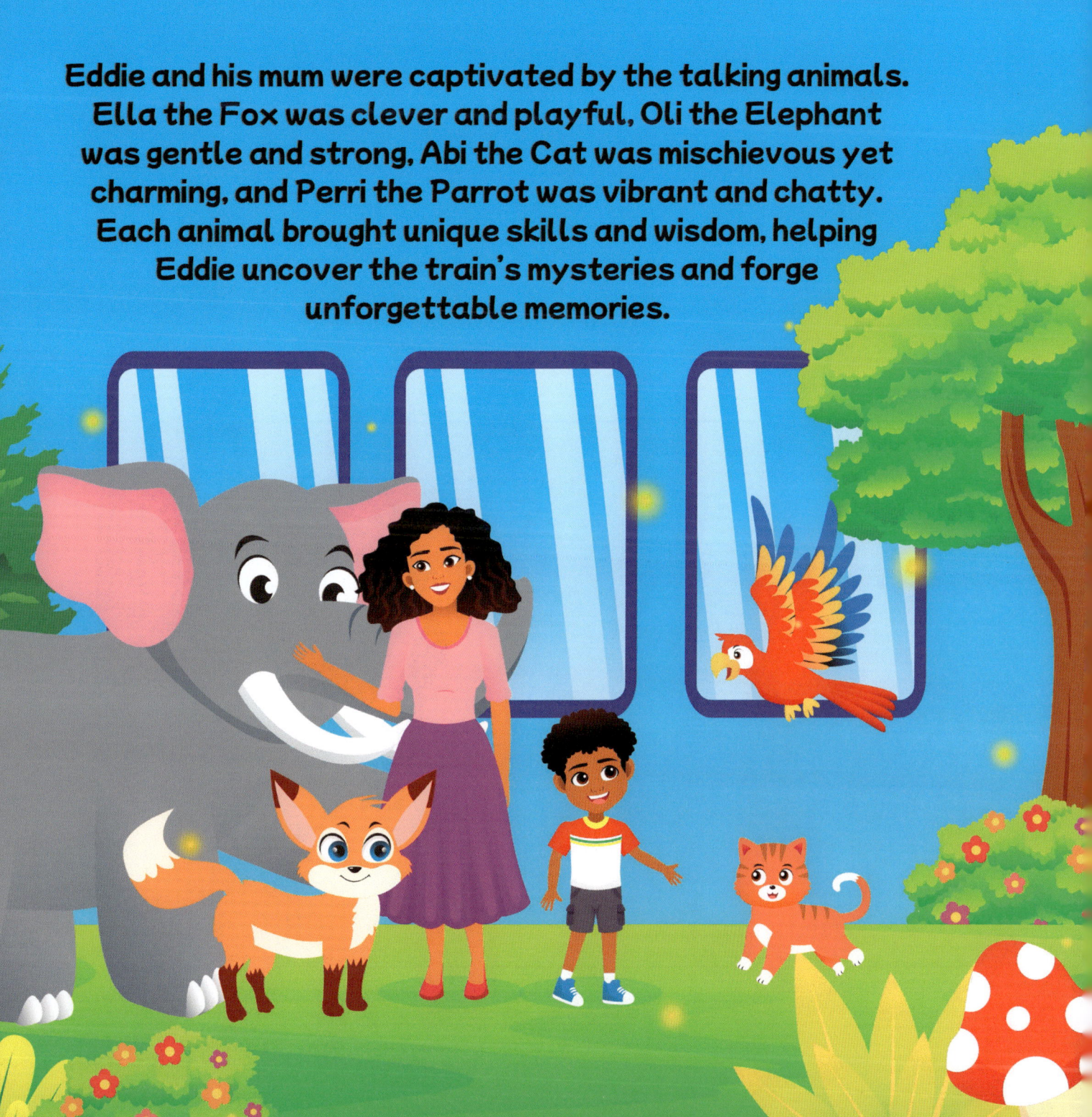

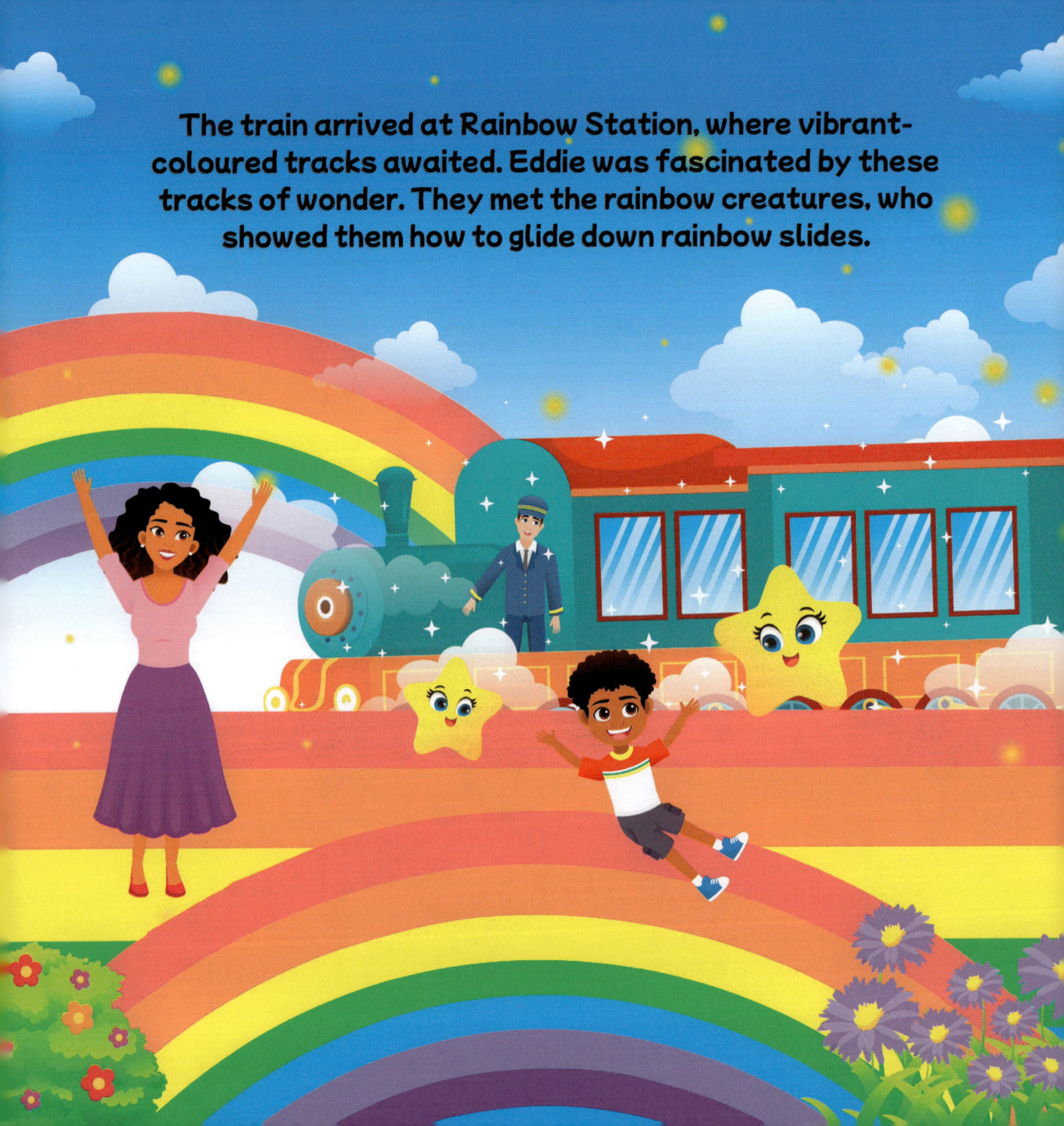

The train arrived at Rainbow Station, where vibrant-coloured tracks awaited. Eddie was fascinated by these tracks of wonder. They met the rainbow creatures, who showed them how to glide down rainbow slides.

Next, the Adventure Express took them to the Land of Giggles, where everyone laughed and played all day. Eddie and Hannah joined a game of giggle tag and couldn't stop laughing at the funny faces everyone made. Eddie was grateful for the incredible friends he made along the way.

Afterwards, they visited the Cloud Castle, high above the skies. Eddie and Hannah met the Cloud King, who invited them to float on fluffy clouds and watch the stars twinkle in the sky.

Their final stop was the Great Train Fair, where trains from around the world gathered. Eddie saw steam engines, high-speed rails, locomotives and trains that played music as they chugged along.

They found Rusty the steam engine at the Great Train fair, just like Eddie's toy but larger than life. Rusty whistled a cheerful hello and rode Eddie and his mum around the fair's railway.

As the adventure continued, Eddie felt a sense of wonder and happiness, a feeling he couldn't describe in words. He and his mum laughed and played, making memories they would never forget.

At sunset, it was time to head back home. Eddie and his mum waved goodbye to the animals, Mr. Conductor and the Adventure Express. They felt sad to leave but were grateful for their fantastic experience.

The Adventure Express settled back into its dusty corner when they returned to the City Transport Museum. Eddie knew he would never forget this day and hoped to revisit the magnificent train soon.

When they arrived home, Eddie looked at his mum and smiled. "Today was the best day of my life! Thank you for coming on the adventure with me. Hannah hugged him tightly. "I had a wonderful time too. Always remember the magic is in our hearts and our dreams."

Eddie's adventure was thrilling; his love for trains led to amazing discoveries and unforgettable friendships. That night, as he snuggled into his train-shaped bed, he closed his eyes and dreamed of the Adventure Express, knowing that with a bit of imagination, new adventures were only a corner away.

THE END

Printed in Great Britain
by Amazon